We have another example of this smoky jazz style on the tune 'You've Changed', recorded as material for *Live At Blues Alley*. Eva's father, Hugh Cassidy, was drawn to 'Still Not Ready' and suggested it for inclusion. The balance of the songs in this book were chosen by Eva.

Those of us who heard her live recognise every other track as Eva's favourites, the ones she was likely to sing for us in those little clubs where she performed.

On Eva Cassidy's web sites one is asked to name a favourite song from Eva's recordings. When I first saw that question, I did not know how to respond. I love so many of her songs for different reasons! The music in this songbook, however, represents many of the 'biggies' on my list. I am so delighted that the world now gets to play and hear Eva's version of 'Danny Boy'. It brings tears to my eyes every time I hear her sing this tune, and I cried again when my husband played Eva's version on the piano. 'Tennessee Waltz' is another of my all-time favourites for some strange reason. I grew up in the 1950s in the US when it was a pop song; and I dare say that most people would not have bet on a revival of this particular song. When I first heard Eva

sing it, I was astounded. It was also on the little cassette tape from Pearls. Eva obviously loved it enough to record it in Chris Biondo's studio for inclusion on her next album. I think Eva will make this a 'classic'. The same scenario holds true for Eva's versions of John Lennon's 'Imagine' and also 'Early Morning Rain' and 'Fever'.

The purpose of a songbook is to share wonderful melodies and lyrics with those who play an instrument and/or sing. This songbook is a treasure, as are the other previously published Eva Cassidy songbooks. Eva's careful selection of material means that every song is 'a winner'! Eva would love the idea that people not only listen to her voice on CD but also value her selection of music and her unique arrangements.

The cover photo of Eva was taken by her cousin Walter Wunderlich on Green Hill in Nova Scotia. Eva and her Mom, Barbara Cassidy, visited family in Pictou, Nova Scotia in 1994. During the visit Walter and Eva took off on Walter's motorcycle and saw wonderful things on that trip.

We include in this introduction other photos from Eva's trip to Nova Scotia. Eva loved the smallest flowers in the fields and would get down on the ground to photograph the tiniest flower, or rock formations, as well as the vistas of beauty she encountered.

The original artwork by Eva Cassidy of the 'Girl With Bee' *(back cover)* was created as a label for jars of honey Eva gave to friends as a Christmas gift and to lift the 'winter blues'. Perhaps a self-portrait, it is a wonderful example of Eva's creativity in her everyday life. Her friends and family still treasure these simple and direct expressions of Eva's love, humour and artistic talent.

On behalf of Eva's parents, Hugh and Barbara Cassidy, her friends and extended family, we wish you many hours of enjoyment with this *Imagine* songbook.

Elana R. Byrd

Among the amazing sights was the beauty of Green Hill and the valley below. Eva, always the artist and concerned with composition, set up this photo of herself. I first saw it in her small three-volume set of photograph albums from that trip. Barbara said to me: 'I think you might like to see these.' At the time we were looking for a picture for another project. When I saw this particular photo, all I could think of was 'Fields Of Gold' but that song and that album *(Songbird)* were already released. Then I met Walter and he described the trip and how much he and Eva shared the joy of observing nature and beautiful sights. Their most amazing experience on that trip was not recorded with a camera. Walter and Eva sat on rocks at the water's edge at Cape John, Nova Scotia one night and watched hundreds of shooting stars while listening to the sounds of night creatures. Eva later told her mother it was one of the most exciting experiences of her life.

Exclusive distributors:
Music Sales Limited
8/9 Frith Street, London W1D 3JB, England.
Music Sales Pty Limited
120 Rothschild Avenue, Rosebery, NSW 2018, Australia.

Order No. AM975722
ISBN 0-7119-9704-7
This book © Copyright 2002 by Wise Publications.

Music arrangements by Jack Long.
Music processed by Paul Ewers Music Design.

Printed in the United Kingdom by
Printwise (Haverhill) Limited, Haverhill, Suffolk.

www.musicsales.com

Your Guarantee of Quality:

As publishers, we strive to produce every book
to the highest commercial standards.

While endeavouring to retain the original running
order of the recorded album, the book has been
carefully designed to minimise awkward page turns
and to make playing from it a real pleasure.

Throughout, the printing and binding have been
planned to ensure a sturdy, attractive publication
which should give years of enjoyment.

If your copy fails to meet our high standards,
please inform us and we will gladly replace it.

It Doesn't Matter Anymore

Words & Music by Paul Anka.

Gol - ly gee, what have you done to me? Well I

guess it does - n't mat - ter a - ny - more.

Ain't no use in me a - cry - - ing 'cause I've

7

now and__ for - ev - er till the end of__ time;__ and I'll find__

some - bo - dy new, ba - by,__ we'll say we're through,_____ and

To Coda ⊕

D.%. al Coda

you won't mat - ter a - ny - more.__

⊕ *Coda*

You won't mat - ter a - ny - more.

Verse 2:
Do you remember, baby, last September how you
Held me tight each and every night?
Woh, baby, how you drove me crazy!
Well I guess it doesn't matter any more.

Who Knows Where The Time Goes?

Words & Music by Sandy Denny.

it was time for them to go.

By the winter fire I will still be

dreaming. I do not count the time,

for who knows where

Verse 2:
Sad deserted shore
Your fickle friends are leaving
Oh but then you know
It was time for them to go
But I will still be here
I have no thought of leaving
I do not count the time
For who knows where the time goes?
Who knows where the time goes?

Verse 3:
I know I'm not alone
While my love is near me
I know that it's so
Until it's time to go
All the storms in winter
And the birds in spring again
I do not count the time
For who knows where the time goes?
Who knows where the time goes?

Fever

Words & Music by John Davenport & Eddie Cooley.

1. Nev - er know how much I love you,
(Verses 2-4 see block lyrics)
you'll nev - er know how____ much I care.____

When you put your arms___ a - round_ me,___ I get a feel-

- ing___ that I just can't_ bear.___ You give me fev - er_____

when you kiss___ me,___ fev - er when you hold___ me tight;

fev - er___ in the morn - ing,___

fev - er all through the night.___

1-3.

4.

You give me fev - er.___

Repeat ad lib. to fade

Verse 2:
Bless my soul, I love you
Take this heart away
Take these arms, I never use them
And just believe what my lips have to say
You give me fever when you kiss me
Fever when you hold me tight
Fever in the morning
Fever all through the night.

Verse 3:
Listen to me, baby
Hear every word I say
No one can love you the way I do
Because they don't know how to love you my way
You give me fever when you kiss me
Fever when you hold me tight
Fever in the morning
Fever all through the night.

Verse 4:
Sun lights up the daytime
The moon lights up at night
My eyes light up when you call my name
Because I know you're gonna treat me right
You give me fever when you kiss me
Fever when you hold me tight
Fever in the morning
Fever all through the night.

You've Changed

Words by Bill Carey.
Music by Carl Fischer.

each me-mo-ry_____ that we shared._____ You ig - nore ev-'ry star

a - bove you.   I can't re - al - ise_____ that you ev - er cared. 3. You've

changed,___
(Verse 5 see block lyric)   you're___ not the ang - el   I once knew.

No___ need to tell me_____ we're through;   it's all ov - er now,___

Verse 5:
You've changed
That sparkle in your eye is gone
And your smile is just a careless yawn
It's all over now
You've changed.

Imagine

Words & Music by John Lennon.

1. Im - ag - ine there's no hea - ven,
(Verses 2-3. see block lyrics)

it's ea - sy if___ you try;___ no hell___ be -

Verse 2:
Imagine there's no countries
It isn't hard to do
Nothing to kill or die for
And no religion too
Imagine all the people living life in peace.

Verse 3:
Imagine no possessions
I wonder if you can
No need for greed or hunger
A brotherhood of man
Imagine all the people sharing all the world.

Still Not Ready

Words & Music By Christian R Izzy & Leo La Sota.

Don't make

30

Early Morning Rain

Words & Music by Gordon Lightfoot.

34

Verse 2:
Out on runway number nine
Big seven-o-seven set to go
But I'm stuck here on the ground
Where the cold winds blow
You can't jump a jet plane
Like you can a freight train
So I'll best be on my way
In the early morning rain.

Verse 3:
Instrumental

Verse 4:
Hear the mighty engines roar
See the silver bird on high
She's away out westward bound
Far above my home she'll fly
Where the morning rain don't fall
And the sun always shines
She'll be flying past my home
In about three hours time.

Verse 5:
In the early morning rain
With a dollar in my hand
And an aching in my heart
And my pockets full of sand
I'm a long way from home
And I miss my loved ones so
In the early morning rain
With no place to go.

Tennessee Waltz

Words & Music by Redd Stewart & Pee Wee King.

I Can Only Be Me

Words & Music by Stevie Wonder.

1. But - ter - flies be - gin _____ from
(Verse 2 see block lyric)

hav - ing been an - oth - er as _____ a child is born _____ from

Verse 2:
Flowers cannot bloom until it is their season
As we would not be here unless it was our destiny
But how many times have you wished to be in spaces
Time, places than what you were
Yet who's to say with unfamiliar faces
You could any more be
Loving you? Can't you see
You can only be you
As I can only be me.

Danny Boy

Trad. Arr. Eva Cassidy.

or when the val - - - - ley's hushed

and white with snow.

'Tis I'll be here in sun - shine or in

sha - - - dow. Oh Dan - ny

Verse 2:
But when ye come in all the roses' falling
And I am dead, as dead I well may be
Go out and find the place where I am lying
And kneel and say an "Ave" there for me
And I will hear the soft sure tread above me
And then my grave will more than sweeter be
For you shall bend and tell me that you love me
And I will sleep in peace until you come to me.

Wayfaring Stranger

Trad. Arr. Eva Cassidy.

sick - - ness, toil or dan - ger_____ in that bright

land_____ to which I_____ go. I'm go - ing

there_____ to see_____ my fa - ther,_____ I'm go - ing

there_____ no more to roam._____ I'm on - ly

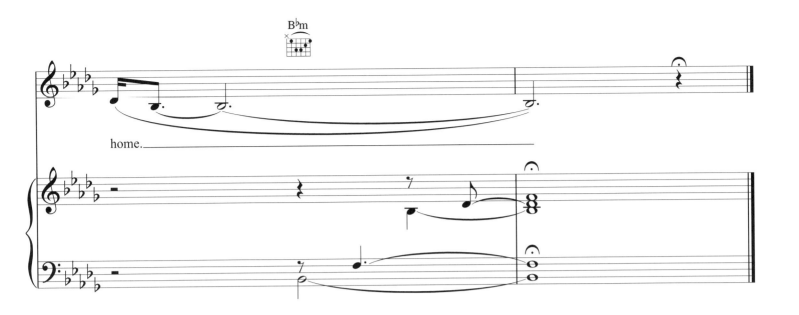

home._____

Verse 2:
I know dark clouds will gather o'er me
I know my way is rough and steep
Yet beautiful fields lie just before me
In that bright land to which they keep.
I'm going there to see my mother
I'm going there no more to roam
I'm only going over Jordan
I'm only going over home.

Verse 3:
I want to wear a crown of glory
When I get home to that good land
I want to shout salvation's story
In concert with the blood-washed band.
I'm going there to see my saviour
I'm going there no more to roam
I'm only going over Jordan
I'm only going over home.

Bold Young Farmer

Trad. Arr. Eva Cassidy.

and____ I____ must con -
- fess____ that I____ love____ him____ still.____
2. I wish,____ I wish, but it's
all____ in____ vain;____ I____

Verse 3:
There sits a bird in yonder tree
Some say he's blind and cannot see
And I wish it was the same with me
Before I took up with your company.

Verse 4:
I wish my babe so tiny was born
And smiling on his father's knee
And I, poor girl, was dead and gone
With the green grass growing all over me.

Verse 5:
Go dig my grave, dig long and deep
Place a marble stone at my head and feet
And on the heart put a snow-white dove
To let the world know that I died for love.